MUSIC IN THE GARDEN OF GOOD AND EVIL

VOLUME I OF III

LORNE LEE, BA, MM

MUSIC IN THE GARDEN OF GOOD AND EVIL

Inner Sound Books

Savannah, Georgia

Manufactured in the United States of America

ISBN 978-0-9801614-0-3

2nd Edition

For my mother, Betty Lee, for my father, H. David Lee, for my grandparents, for my inspirational sister, Lorriana, and for the Lee and Johnson Family. I come from the deep roots of a proud tree planted by living waters.

Table of Contents

INTRODUCTION

MUSIC HAS BEEN CENTRAL TO HUMAN LIFE FOR THOUSANDS OF years, awakening as nothing else can the emotions of joy and peace.

Music in the Garden of Good and Evil is the story of the purpose of music and the deleterious effects music can have on you if the door of musical responsibility is left unguarded. Although the story I tell here is fictional, the principles that underlie it are very real and of great consequence for your life.

I hope you enjoy the message. If you find the story important, then tell others to read this book. If music is so important to our lives, then is it not important enough to understand how it works? Even for those who have no musical background, understanding the divine plan for music is essential for your life. And yes, you will see why very soon.

We are all aware of how we are influenced by our family, friends, and leaders. These influences impact our lives and structure our beliefs. For instance, all of us are familiar with the City of Kings and the dangers that lurk therein. I am sure you have been warned many times about the city, the people who live there, and how they are full of everything but true happiness. Have you ever wondered why the our forefathers have been so careful to warn us of the music in this place?

Then come, sit at my table, and get comfortable. Let me share with you this cup of musical *TRUTH*, so that you, too, may understand what it means for your mind to be refreshed by living *waters*.

CHAPTER 1

ONCE UPON AN ANCIENT TIME THERE LIVED three travelers named Tad, Menik, and Otto. The three friends were from a small village just a day's journey from the City of Kings. All of their lives Tad, Menik, and Otto had been protected from the influences of the City of Kings and the dangers that lurked therein, for the city was full of confused people. The people who lived there were full of material wealth, but they were not full of happiness. Sadly enough, *Music* and *Words* did not live in *Unity* and *Harmony*.

Nobody knew why.
Nobody thought to try.
As long as the music was made to please people,
Nobody seemed to cry.

The Music Ministers of the city had discovered a special blend of music that kept people...well... somewhat happy. They declared: To be a good citizen you must listen only to the music that we provide.

Now, Tad, Menik, and Otto had grown up sharing a powerful dream of uniting beautiful music with inspirational words. They thought upon this dream so much that the dream began to grow and grow. The dream grew until the day had come when the three friends set out on that very quest: FIND INSPIRING MUSIC FOR THEIR INSPIRING WORDS.

In their quest for musical splendor, the travelers encountered a gray-haired wise man, the Prophet. They explained to the Prophet that they were on a quest to discover a way to unite inspiring music with inspiring words.

The Prophet listened carefully, and then replied, "Young men, to find the roots of what you seek you must go to the Garden!"

"The Garden? The Garden? What Garden?" The travelers were in great confusion. "Thank you, kind sir. But with all due respect, we are travelers in search of music, not gardening," Tad explained.

"But wait! I have a word for you." The Prophet walked closer and placed his hand on Otto's shoulder. "Out of the garden will be released within you the secrets of music. These secrets will bless the world with the wisdom of the ONE TRUE SOUND. *Knock and the door shall be opened; seek and ye shall find; ask and it shall be given.* Go to the Garden of Good and Evil and the gardener will direct thy path. I am a prophet of music, follower of the teachings of the garden. Peace be unto you."

Then the wise man turned around, kicked the dust

from his sandals, and began to walk away.

Otto felt truth in the prophet's words. "Sir."

The prophet did not reply.

"Sir, Sir, Sir!!! We believe you! Please tell us where to find the garden," said Otto in the most humble voice he could manage in his excitement. "Do we follow the path to the city?"

The prophet slowly turned around, looked Otto in the eyes, and said, "You already know the way. You all have recited the sacred map since you were children: *Yea, though I walk through the Valley of the Shadow of Death and cross the Sea of Reeds (the Red Sea), I shall look to the hills from which cometh my help.* The Garden of Good and Evil sits on top of the tallest hill. The journey is long, but the rewards are far greater. May wisdom be a lamp unto thy feet and a light unto thy pathway. Go in peace and find what you seek."

"Thank you," replied the travelers.

And with the words of a wise man in their hearts, the three young travelers set off on their journey to reach the garden. On the way they were subjected to many trials. They crossed desert valley sands, waded through treacherous waters, and climbed steep mountains in pursuit of their goal.

The travelers even began to question whether or not their search would be successful. But just as their spirits were plunging into despair, low and behold, they saw before them the most beautiful golden gates.

They wondered in amazement: *could these be the gates to the Garden of Good and Evil?*

The Garden of Good and Evil held all of the fruits of sound and all of the secrets of music. All of the music on earth grew out of the Garden of Good and Evil. The seeds were planted by the Creator and cared for by the gardener.

The power and mysteries of the garden drew people from all over the world. Everyone wanted to learn the secrets of music. The problem was that many people used the sound-fruit of the garden for the wrong reasons.

Many people believed the myth that by eating the fruit of the garden, the secrets of music would be released into their body. Some did not care about the secrets themselves, they just wanted to get their hands on the sound-fruit and make music as fast as they could.

Only a few of these seekers ever really learned the secrets of music. You see, many people have entered the garden, but few had bothered to ask the gardener how the fruits of sound were made. Ah yes, this gardener knew the secrets of the Garden of Good and Evil.

The gardener's name was Percy. He was a humble fellow with a hump on his back and the hands of a laborer. Nobody bothered Percy, because Percy appeared harmless.

But Percy was wise— wise enough to know that the secret knowledge held within the garden was not for everyone to know. He knew that music came a responsibility many people knew nothing about. And he also knew that many travelers who had entered the garden were not ready to receive the secrets of the garden.

For years Percy had observed travelers seeking the secrets of the garden. Such travelers plucked and consumed the fruit. They made music to please themselves without ever learning all of the wonderful ways the fruit were intended to be used. These people never experienced the power of the sound-fruit.

CHAPTER 2

As Tad, Menik, and Otto approached the garden, a gatekeeper stepped forward to challenge them.

"Will you use the fruits of sound in the Spirit of Truth?" The gatekeeper asked in a bold voice. The travelers all said that the Spirit of Truth was precisely what they had longed for in music.

They began to feel their bodies swaying to the rhythms of the fruit-filled trees and the gentle hymns of the whistling winds.

"Then enter," the gatekeeper replied, "but I must warn you: *NEVER EAT OF THE FRUIT!*"

The garden was massive. Rows and rows of fruit trees stretched as far as the eye could see. The garden was very orderly and lovingly cared for. Baskets were placed under each tree to harvest the fruit.

After walking deeper into the garden, the travelers saw an old man on his knees pulling weeds. "This must be the gardener." They eagerly approached to introduced themselves.

"We are travelers seeking to unite our divinely inspired words with beautiful music. My name is Tad. I write words of strength and victory."

The next traveler approached to greet. "My name is Menik. I write words of inspiration that can bring people out of sadness and pain."

The last traveler stepped forward. "My name is Otto, and I write inspirational words of joy and happiness!"

The gardener stood tall and smiled at the travelers. "It's very good to meet you all. My name is Percy, and I am the gardener. I hope you will enjoy your visit to the Garden of Good and Evil."

Percy stooped again and returned to his work. "I must get back to tending the garden," he explained. Then Percy looked up one last time to give a warning. "Beware of the snake, my friends. You know that a snake in a garden always spells trouble." He laughed and turned his attention back to the few weeds remaining in the patch before him.

"You are right. Such a snake might even tempt me with the an apple!" The travelers began to laugh.

But the gardener became serious and repeated his warning. "Beware of the snake. You know that a snake in a garden always spells trouble."

CHAPTER 3

Tad and Menik began to walk toward the fruit trees with the baskets they had picked up at the front gate. But Otto decided to follow Percy and watch the love and care the gardener gave to each piece of fruit. He saw the detail in Percy's gardening.

"How does the garden work?" Otto asked.

Percy looked up at Otto. "Well, it works like this. The fruit in the garden have the power of good and evil. Just as the power of life and death is in the tongue, the power of joy and pain is inside the fruit of the garden. The sound-fruit are not evil, nor are they good. They are merely a reflection of the will of the person releasing the sound into the air."

Percy rose to his feet and began pacing back and forth. "Now let us take, for example, the creation of light. When the earth was created, it was dark. Now what happened to create light?"

"The creator said, 'Let there be light!' Then light come to be," Otto answered.

"Exactly!" Percy exclaimed. "A word was spoken, and everything blossomed into light. With a word the world was flooded with light. And some people doubt there is the power of life and death in the tongue?"

Percy paused to listen to the wind moving through the trees like wind chimes. "Now, what is something that all words have in common?"

"Is it that all words are sounds?" Otto asked in confusion.

Percy looked at Otto, as if Otto did not understand the power of his own words. "Yes," he said. "The Creator spoke into darkness and made light with the sounds of words. This is also the way all sound-fruit respond. The sound-fruit were placed here by the Creator to represent all that life can be. But remember, never to eat the fruit. The fruit of sound enters the body through the ears, not the mouth. This fruit is not like other fruit. Just as the power of life and death is in the tongue, so is the power of joy and pain in the sound-fruit of the garden. There are only a few types of fruit, but the flavors change by the way you combine them with words."

"Wait a minute," said Otto. "How can the flavor change?"

"The fruit by themselves are sounds that bend to the will of words. But the sounds can only bend so far. Each sound-fruit has a different taste. Let me show you." Percy pointed to a sweetly ripened piece of fruit hanging from a tree.

Percy stared at the fruit, as if the fruit were looking back at him. "Now this fruit is a major sound-fruit.

Although it is not much to look at, this fruit is shaped for joy, happiness, and love."

Percy gave Otto time to absorb his words. "Listen carefully, Otto. This is the exciting part!" Percy then held the sound-fruit in his right hand, and with excitement said, "MY HEART IS FULL OF JOY!"

Suddenly the fruit became soft and round. It glowed the most beautiful shade of sunshine yellow and clear sky blue.

"Now behold, the beauty of sound!" Percy exclaimed. Otto heard the mysteries of the ages in the voice of Percy. And then it happened. The major sound-fruit blossomed into a pure, glowing sound. It was the most beautiful sound that Otto had ever heard. It was the sound of pure joy. It was not joy filtered through the world. It was *pure joy*, just as nature had intended!

Otto stood in amazement. He could not believe what he was hearing and seeing. As he stood in shock and awe, Percy picked another sound-fruit from the same tree. With the fruit held higher in the air, he said the word, *Love*, with love in his heart.

Suddenly the fruit became a beautiful, calming shade of orange with a fuzzy, peach-like feel. It reminded Otto of the pure, selfless love a mother has for her child. *Love is patient. Love is kind.*

"Now listen." Percy took a deep breath. When he closed his eyes, the major sound-fruit blossomed into pure sound. But it was not the sound Otto had heard before. This was the pure sound of love. Otto began to smile, because the sound went into his ears, through his body, and touched his heart.

"How can these things happen?" Otto said in amazement. "How can sound touch my heart and make me feel loved?"

"Ancient wisdom tells us: The good treasure of the heart bringeth forth good things,'" Percy responded. "Now there is love in your heart. So when you make music, the music will know love. Out of the heart the mouth speaks, and out of the heart the music flows. Now love will flow out of your music."

"Amazing, Percy! Please teach me the secrets of the garden," Otto humbly begged.

THE GOOD TREASURE OF THE HEART BRINGETH FORTH GOOD THINGS

CHAPTER 4

Percy spoke to Otto carefully, as though he were measuring the importance of each word. "There is only one way to learn the musical secrets of the garden. You must roll up your sleeves and become a *gardener*. What you need to know is down there...in the soil...at the root of the sound. You must care for the sound-fruit trees, protect them from weeds and vines, and nurture them, so that the heart of the listener can enjoy the sweet nectar of pure sound. Are you willing to work for me, an old gardener?" Percy asked.

Otto shouted his answer, as if the garden had ears. "My purpose in life is to bring forth joy and happiness through music! Anything that might bring more joy to the world I will do. Maybe if I learn the secrets of music, I can bring more joy than ever!"

"Well then, let us begin," Percy replied. And with that confirmation, he pointed to the shovel and the dry ground, and said, "Start digging."

"Digging?" Otto was surprised and confused.

"You said that you wanted to learn the secrets of the garden, did you not?" Percy asked.

"Yes, this is true," Otto replied in, a puzzled tone.

"Then start digging," said Percy. "To be able to understand the fruit, you must know its roots. To understand the roots, you must know the purpose of the seed. And to understand its purpose, you must know the person who planted the seed. I plant the seeds, for I am the gardener. If you want to know me, then grab a shovel and start digging. The divine secrets of music are given those dedicated enough to bear their own shovels and follow me."

CHAPTER 5

The Garden of Good and Evil held many challenges for the untrained gardener. It takes an experienced gardener, like Percy, to teach someone how to plant and care for the fruit trees of the garden. Nobody knows how Percy got the job as gardener, but as long as the garden has been there, so has he.

"You know, Otto, believing cometh by hearing," Percy declared. "Since music is something to be heard, let us make sure you understand the nature of the sounds that you hear. It just may have a bearing on what you believe. There are just four things you need to know about the music of Good and Evil:

The Purpose of the Sound-Fruit
The Blossoming of the Sound-Fruit
The Combining of the Fruit
The Path and Alignment of Music

"Let us begin our discussion with the purpose of each sound-fruit. The purpose of the sound-fruit is to blossom into sound that has the power to touch the heart of man. Each of the kinds of fruit has its own characteristics. This is known as the *Lessons of the Five Fruit.* When words are spoken into sound-fruit, the sound-fruit blossom into pure living sound."

Percy then looked at Otto with a smile, and asked, "Otto, you do not suppose the people are speaking words into the sound-fruit without knowing which fruit match the words, do you?"

"I am most sure of it, Percy," Otto replied "Percy, you are a very wise and funny man. People may be speaking words of joy into sounds of doom."

"Precisely! Then is it possible that internal conflicts in such music could be causing the listener to miss out on their musical blessing?" Percy asked. "It is written to give one-tenth of your increase to the storehouse, or you will be counted a thief and a curse be put upon your head. How good would it be to have robbed people of the musical blessings just because you did not take *one-tenth* of your the time to study music?"

"That would make me a thief, and I do not want to be the thief!" Otto replied in fear. "I know that a lack of knowledge does not shield me from responsibility. I would like to study to show myself approved. So please teach me the *Lessons of the Five Fruit.*"

Percy spoke with an encouraging tone. "My friend, if you are *so* intent on finding the truth behind music, then you may come with me in the morning to the center of the garden and hear a lesson." And full of anticipation, Otto rushed off to bed.

BELIEVING COMETH BY HEARING

Chapter 6

A peaceful day had just dawned in the Garden of Good and Evil. The fruit on the trees were glowing with all of the colors of the rainbow, and the garden was full of their fragrance.

Percy was awakened by the sounds the birds singing. After getting dressed, he joined an eagerly waiting Otto on the banks of the river that flowed near the center of the garden.

Percy resumed his lesson. "From the moment the sound-fruit is held in your hand and you speak life into it, the fruit blossoms into pure sound. At that moment the fruit is in a state of *becoming*. When the pure sound is released into the air, the pure sound is in a state of *being*— being what it is meant to be. The fruit were designed with a purpose in mind. But unlike many people, the fruit have known their purpose and live that purpose *without compromise* every day."

After this preamble, Percy continued his instruction. "Now, Otto, there is a time in a person's life when he finds happiness. This happiness fills the heart with joy, love, victory, and celebration. The sound is sweet to the ear. This sound is comes from a major sound-fruit (Now we call it a major chord). When words are applied to a major sound-fruit, that fruit blossoms into a sound that takes on a life based upon the words of life you speak into it."

"Like when light entered the world?" Otto asked.

"Exactly," Percy responded. "And when you are making music that is filled from start to finish with major sound-fruit, then the major sound-fruit becomes the foundation of your song. The center message of such a song can be joy, love, victory, or good.

"The other sound-fruit blossom in the same way. Minor sound-fruit can fill the heart with pain, anguish, trial, death, sadness, and mourning. When you are making music that is filled from start to finish with minor sound-fruit, then the minor sound-fruit becomes the center of the foundation of your song. The center message of that song can be pain, sadness, mourning, or evil.

"Transition sound-fruit (dominant chords) can fill the heart with a sense of transitioning through life. This type of change is a positive change. The function of this sound-fruit is to show the transition from one point to another. It transitions one sound to another."

The transition sound-fruit were changing shapes from round like a ball to square like a box. The colors were new with each shape. "Yes, the transition fruit is an unstable sound. You will have fun with that one."

Percy pulled two other fruit from the trees. "There are two other kinds of transition sound-fruit. One of these transition sound-fruit is the 'altered sound-fruit.' This sound-fruit can fill the heart with a sense of transitioning through the trials of life into times of hardship. This type of change is a negative change, but can suddenly turn positive. The function of this sound-fruit is also to show the transition from one point to another. But it mostly transitions any sound into a minor sound.

"The last transition sound-fruit is the confusion sound-fruit (diminished chords). This fruit can fill the heart with a sense of confusion or terror. This type of change is a negative change. The function of this sound-fruit is to show the transition from one point to another. It transforms any sound to another sound."

One by one, Percy began to speak while holding the fruit. Each of the sound-fruit blossomed into its own, unique sound.

"I see, Percy," Otto remarked. "You are saying that all music is made up of five sound-fruit: Major, Minor, Dominant, Altered, and Diminished. Then these sound-fruit blossom into sound."

Immediately Percy responded. "Yes, Otto, these are the five different sound-fruit. Now, what makes the sound-fruit become music is that the sounds are traveling in a direction. Music with direction is powerful. With a sense of direction, music twists and turns like the path to a village. Combining the fruit is the most well-known way to make music here in the garden. It is not the only way, but it is a great way to make music."

MUSIC WITH DIRECTION IS POWERFUL. MUSIC TWISTS AND TURNS LIKE THE PATH TO A VILLAGE.

CHAPTER 7

AFTER A FEW WEEKS OF TRAINING, PERCY GAVE OTTO TEN tablets on which were written the secrets of sound combination. Here I will interrupt my fable to share as much as I can of the tablets with you. Portions of these tablets are written in ancient musical code. *Do not let your mind become heavy by the parts of the tablets that are beyond your understanding.* Walk forward through the golden doors of these ancient words and you will be given wisdom beyond measure.

Also, keep in mind that over the years wars and rumors of wars throughout the world have kept these tablets separated. The famous ten tablets were said to have been lost sometime during the eleventh century. Only seven of them were recovered.

THE TEN TABLETS

Tablet 1
Doctrine of Sound Combination

COMBINING SOUND-FRUIT is the next step to making music. This is done by matching words to the proper piece of fruit. Once you match the fruit with the words, the song will be in agreement.

There are twelve levels for every kind of sound-fruit (C-C#-D-E♭-E-F-F#-G-A♭-A-B♭-B, the twelve notes). Raise the fruit higher or lower to move between levels. Use the sound-fruit in a way that maintains stability.

The level one major sound-fruit (C Major Chord) moves with stability to the level six (F Major Chord) or eight major sound-fruit (G Major Chord).

The level one major sound-fruit (C Major Chord) moves with stability to the level three, five, or ten minor sound-fruit (The D, E, and A Minor Chords). But the level one major sound-fruit moves in chaos to the level five, seven, and ten major sound-fruit (E, F#, and A Major Chords). The reverse is also true.

Otto gave Percy the strangest look. His face turned into a question mark of some kind. Otto scratched his head and kicked the dirt. He was completely lost.

"I don't get it! What do levels have to do with music? This is confusing," said Otto in frustration.

"It only confuses you because the biggest secret anyone can have is the secret that stares you in the face. You see Otto, many people hear these secrets all the time. It surprises me that they are still secret. Why do you think this is true?"

"Ah, I get it!" Otto exclaimed. "These secrets are not meant to be secrets. They are *meant* to be understood. Please help me understand this tablet."

Percy saw that Otto was eager to learn and was pleased. So Percy talked more about the first tablet.

"The first tablet," he explained, "is definitely the most confusing one. Here it is. Music moves by raising the fruit to one of twelve levels and choosing a path. Imagine all of the paths from the Valley of Shadows to the City of Kings. You can choose the main path, the unexpected path, the deceptive path, or the dangerous paths. All of these paths lead to the City of Kings. But the question is: *On which path do you choose to have your loved ones travel?* The royal road signs will tell you which paths are safe. The main path is the safe path. This is a path that a person would take if they were seeking peace. If you are seeking unexpected sights, you might want to choose another path. The main path leads you directly to the City of Kings. This tablet is saying that certain sound-fruit will take you on a direct path from one sound to another, while keeping you at peace. Others paths may not. Let us look at the next tablet."

Tablet 2

IF YOU MOVE FROM a level eight transition sound-fruit (G Major/Minor 7th Chord) to a level nine major sound-fruit (A♭ Major Chord), the result will be a deceptive movement. This is a chord of peace, love, and joy being used deceptively, disguised as the main path. This is an example of the most deceptive of all the sounds in the Garden. The fruits are not evil, but the way you use them can be.

The movement of completion is essential if the listener is ever able to feel the sense of completion that may be missing from their lives. A song that is moving towards completion will flow like a river from a transition sound-fruit to a major sound-fruit.

Tablet 3

THERE ARE TWO THINGS that are near and dear to my heart— the suspension sound-fruit (a variation of the transition sound-fruit) and the movement of modulation. A suspension sound-fruit will bring to the heart a building feeling of hope. It is quite amazing. It is known in my land as the *Sound of Faith*.

The most uplifting movement of any fruit is the upward modulation. The fruit will climb by either one or two levels. The result is that the original feeling of the sound-fruit will now be doubled. Love will become greater love, peace will become greater peace, and joy will become greater joy.

Tablet 4

MUSIC IS LIKE THE WIND. It is directional. It blows from the north, lifts from the south, pushes from the east, and pulls from the west. Imagine a boat in the ocean. The boat can sail with the wind or against the wind. You have powerful oars that you can use to row against the wind. These oars are your message. But wait! Isn't your message directional, too? Isn't your message leading you somewhere? If your message is, in fact, leading you somewhere, then you must make sure that the sounds within the music are not leading the listener in the wrong direction.

Level one, six, and eight major sound-fruit have the same wind direction as level three, five, and ten minor sound-fruit. They also have the same direction as level eight transition and suspension sound-fruit. Deceptive winds push from the side. Interestingly enough, the creator of music always has free will to choose any wind at any time.

KNOW THE WINDS, FOR THIS IS THE NATURE OF MUSIC.

Tablet 5

ONE AREA OF YOUR life to work on is your mind. Your mind is the battleground on which all wars are waged. Music is created by the thoughts of sound in the mind of the musician. Like the stars in the sky, music could have just been placed into existence. But music waits on your thoughts to release it from its cocoon like a butterfly. *Music has wings of sound to lift you.*

Love may inspire music, but ultimately music is a choice. Music is an outpouring of your thoughts. Your thoughts are there before the music is. Since the Evil One knows about the musical choices you can make with your mind, he tries to attack you through your thoughts. If he can control your thoughts, he can control your music. If the Evil One controls your music, he will affect the thousands who will hear it. So I ask, *Who is in control of you?*

Tablet 6

REMEMBER THIS! No man can block music from his mind. It will touch the deepest parts of anyone it reaches. There is no wall of the mind strong enough to keep it out. You cannot reason with music anymore than you can reason with the wind. Music has the power to affect anyone it touches—for good or for evil. Know that there are three things you can do to offset the unwanted effects of music:

Do not listen to it.
Be careful what you listen to.
Think and speak against wrong or conflicting messages.

Tablet 7

THE THIRD OPTION is best. The first two options often limit our lives to the point of fear. Yes, you want to be careful. But when you live in the city, you often hear music that you did not plan to hear. If you hear music that is unhealthy to the spirit, your knowledge will allow you to make a choice to:

- Leave the area
- Speak the pure and peaceful words to combat impure thoughts

CHAPTER 8

Percy spoke to Otto about how many people chose not to listen. "You know, Otto," he said, "some people have found that music causes so many problems that they declared only certain music should be listened to by those who wish to remain whole and righteous. While those people are not necessarily wrong, could they be missing out on a musical blessing? These critics often condemn music when it makes them feel uneasy. But these people are correct in one very important matter."

"What is it?" Otto asked.

"The most important matter in music," said Percy.

"What? What is it?" Otto questioned excitedly.

"The number one thing never to forget," replied Percy.

"Yes, Yes!" Otto shouted, as if he were a ten year-old about to discover the end of a rainbow.

"The most important thing is that music can move the spirit!" Percy explained.

"Music can do what? Move the spirit? I do not understand. Please explain this one to me!"

So Percy expanded on his earlier comments by. "A

series of major sounds followed by an abrupt change to minor sounds can have an affect on the spirit. The spirit within a person may change or move with the sound. So be aware that an abrupt change of sound changes the spirit."

"Tell me more, Percy!" Otto pleaded.

Percy looked calmly at Otto. "In due time. But now it is time to prune the garden."

So Percy began to prune the trees. Otto quickly joined Percy. He rolled up his sleeves and began to pull the weeds.

After five days of pulling weeds had passed, Percy looked down at Otto, and asked, "Well, now do you understand."

"Understand what?" Otto asked.

"Understand why some people only sing and play the songs that they know rather than making new songs," replied Percy.

"No, I don't!" Otto said in disbelief.

"What if I told you that you really did not have to pull all of those weeds?" Percy asked.

"I would be very angry. For my hands are blistered and hurting from this work," Otto said in anger.

"Well, why did you pull these weeds?" Percy asked.

"Because that is what you are supposed to do as a gardener. You pull weeds to protect your fruit. I am just being a good gardener. I saw weeds, so I pulled them," Otto replied.

Percy posed another question. "What if I told you those were not weeds that you were pulling?"

"But if those were not weeds, what were they?" Otto was more puzzled than ever.

Percy replied, "Those were actually the beginning of a sound-fruit bush. Not all fruit grows on trees."

"Please forgive me! I did not know. I did not understand," said Otto in an apologetic tone.

Percy replied, "Like most people who do not understand, you felt it was necessary to remove it. Many people have found great music to celebrate life with. But that is just it. Many do not fully realize what they have found. They put beautiful sounds together without understanding how the sounds work together.

"Sounds have a working relationship with one another. The different sounds that come together have meanings in line with truth only when they are in line with the words of truth." As soon as the last word was out of Percy's mouth, he again turned his attention to the tending of the garden.

DIFFERENT SOUNDS THAT COME TOGETHER HAVE MEANINGS IN LINE THE MUSIC WHEN THE SOUNDS ARE IN LINE WITH THE WORDS THAT INSPIRED THE MUSIC

This was the way of the studies of Otto. For more than a year, Percy gave a wealth of musical secrets to Otto (far too many secrets to list in this book. You will learn more of the secrets another time. But for now, let us move on with our story).

CHAPTER 9

Night had fallen on the Garden, and Otto was very tired from a hard day of labor.

"Eat the fruit", a voice whispered. "Sssssss . . . . Eat the fruit and you will know the secretssssss of the Garden of Good and Evil."

"Who goes there?" Otto looked all around.

"That is not the question you should be asking," the voice replied. "The real question is how you can learn the secrets of the Garden."

"How do you know what I seek?" Otto demanded in an angry voice.

At that moment silence fell upon the area. All you could hear was the hissing of a snake, as it slithered through the grass.

Otto could now see the snake moving closer. As he looked down, Otto was shocked by the fact that a snake was actually talking to him.

"Please do not take offense to my request." The snake spoke in a friendly voice. "I was the Chief Musician for the Creator, and I had to know all of the secrets of music. But before I was kicked out of my Master's house, I learned a way to get all of the secrets of music very quickly. Would you like to know how?"

"Yes," Otto replied. "But how is it that I, a mere gardener's apprentice, could learn the secrets of music so quickly? My hands are tired from working in the field and the gardener gives me little rest."

The snake responded. "All you have to do is to eat of the fruit. By eating the sound-fruit, your mind will become filled with pure musical thoughts."

"I will think long and hard about it, my slithery friend. But if I do indeed eat of the fruit, I will wait for the morning to do so," Otto skeptically replied.

"Then I will meet you here in the morning." The snake hissed and quickly slithered away into the forest.

CHAPTER 10

UPON SEEING PERCY, OTTO SAID, "I WAS VISITED by a snake in the garden after a long day of labor. He said that if I would just eat the fruit, I would know all the secrets of music."

"Do not dare eat of the fruit!" Percy shouted. "If you do, you will become a soul *trapped* in sound to be used by the snake. To eat of the fruit is forbidden. Otto, you have just met the *Original Garden Snake*."

"Thank you for the warning. I surely do not want the snake to possess my soul," Otto said, in the tone of a student in the presence of a respected teacher.

"There are no shortcuts to learning the secrets of music here in the Garden of Good and Evil. You must have patience," Percy declared.

"I understand. I will not again be so foolish as to listen to a snake," promised Otto.

"Good, Otto. Now have some dinner, and let's talk no more about such foolishness." So Percy and Otto shared a meal of grain and vegetables.

THERE ARE NO SHORTCUTS TO THE SECRETS OF MUSIC IN THE GARDEN OF GOOD AND EVIL

CHAPTER 11

Percy was now ready to pass along the proverbial words of wisdom, words that have shaped the changing face of music for thousands of years.

"Otto, for the past year you have been a diligent student. You have studied to show yourself approved. Now it is time for you to learn the Parables of the Garden of Good and Evil."

Then Percy handed Otto a bundle of carefully wrapped papers withered by the hands of time. "Learn the lessons you find on these scrolls. Let the scrolls bring clarity where there is confusion."

And Otto began to read.

The Parables of Music

Music can disturb the spirit by a sudden change in sound. A deer grazing in a pasture is a peaceful animal. At the point of nutritional satisfaction, the deer knows nothing but fulfillment and joy. Suddenly a hungry wolf appears. When the deer

SENSES THE DANGER OF THE WOLF, THE DEER'S JOY TURNS INTO FEAR. THE DEER RUNS AWAY, JUST AS THE SPIRIT OF JOY RUNS AWAY FROM OUR HEARTS WHEN WE HEAR THE MUSIC OF DEATH AND PAIN.

POWERFUL WORDS CAN OVERCOME THE SOUNDS IN MUSIC. BUT IN DOING SO, THEY MUST STRUGGLE, LIKE A MAN SWIMMING AGAINST A POWERFUL CURRENT.

THESE PRINCIPLES OF MUSIC ARE LIKE THE PRINCIPLES OF YOUR DAILY LIFE. EITHER YOU LIVE BY THE PRINCIPLES OF GOOD OR THE WHIMS OF YOUR FLESH. MUSIC WILL BEND TO THE PART OF YOU THAT IS STRONGER. IF YOU ARE NOT STEADY IN THIS UNDERSTANDING, YOUR MUSIC WILL BE AS INCONSISTENT AND LIMITED AS YOUR DAILY LIFE. ANCIENT WISDOM TELLS US TO BE EITHER HOT OR COLD. IF YOU ARE LUKEWARM, YOU WILL BE SPIT OUT OF THE MOUTH OF RIGHTEOUSNESS.

MUSIC IS LIKE A MIGHTY RIVER. IF YOU UNDERSTAND THE DIRECTIONS OF THE CURRENTS, THEN YOU CAN GUIDE THE BOAT (THE LISTENER) TO ITS DESTINATION (THE MESSAGE). YOUR MUSIC IS ALWAYS GUIDING THE LISTENER TO THE RIVER BANKS OF YOUR MESSAGE.

PEACE AT THE RIVER

THINK OF A WOMAN OF BEAUTY AND RADIANCE, AS SHE SITS ON A ROCK BESIDE A CALM RIVER. OVERLOOKING THE BANK WHERE SHE SITS IS A WATERFALL. SHE IS AS PEACEFUL AS A SLEEPING BABY. THINK OF THE PEACEFULNESS WITHIN HER. NOW IMAGINE THERE ARE INNOCENT CHILDREN UNDER HER FEET IN PAIN FROM DISEASE AND FAMINE. CAN YOUR SOUL NOW FORGET THE DYING CHILDREN AND GO BACK TO THE PEACE OF THE WOMAN? OF COURSE NOT. BUT ISN'T THIS WHAT HAPPENS WHEN YOU PLACE SOUNDS OF PAIN UNDER THE WORDS OF PEACE?

GOOD INTENTIONS ALONE DO NOT PROMISE YOU A GOOD LIFE, JUST AS IT DOES NOT PROMISE YOU GOOD MUSIC.

SEARCH YOUR HEART AND MAKE SURE IT IS IN LINE WITH THE WILL OF TRUTH. AS THE WORDS OF THE HEART LINE UP WITH THE WILL OF TRUTH, SO SHALL MUSIC BE IN LINE WITH THE WORDS OF A SONG. IF THE WORDS OF A SONG LINE UP WITH THE WILL OF TRUTH, THEN SO SHALL YOUR MUSIC BE IN LINE WITH TRUTH. MEDITATE ON THESE WORDS DAY AND NIGHT.

The Nature of Sound

What are sounds? Sounds are vibrations in the air. Sounds are like ripples in the water. If you throw a pebble, the ripple will be small and shallow (high sounds). If you throw a large stone, the ripple will be big and deep (low sounds). The impact of the stone will determine how far the ripple travels. Throw a stone in water and also listen to the splash— a high pitched splash for a pebble and a low splash for a large stone. This, too, is the nature of sound.

CHAPTER 12

"Otto, now you are ready to go out into the world and teach people about the good and evil of music," said Percy. "You are now the Chief Music Teacher. Your title will represent your new life as a giver of musical knowledge. Be humble and understand that people are not misusing music out of bad intentions, they are just doing what they feel is right. Remember, many may have great celebration in their hearts but are limited by their traditions. Many will try to break their tradition with whatever the world has to offer. But you will offer much more. You will offer freedom. You will offer *the* knowledge the will free their music."

After a long goodbye, Otto left the garden and set out to share the secrets of the Garden with the world. The center of the known world at this time was the City of Narcis. This was a city full of egos that were overgrown, because their music was the most loved in the known world.

Upon entering the City of Narcis, Otto encountered his old friends Menik and Tad. After exchanging greetings, Otto said, "It seems as if ages have passed since we have seen one another. It has been one year to be exact. How have you been since our separation in the Garden of Good and Evil?"

"Well, to tell you the truth, our lives have been really good. We spread our music throughout the city, and the people love our new songs. We do not know why, but they love it!" Tad exclaimed.

"I am very happy for your new-found success. You know, I have studied the secrets of the Garden of Good and Evil for the past year with the gardener you know as Percy. He taught me this: PEOPLE FLOCK TO WHAT IS NEW, BUT THEY CONNECT TO THE TRUTH. The truth is the core of the music, and the message is what that core is communicating to the listener's soul. Is not that the truth? Will your music stand the test of truth or even the lofty test of time? Obviously the music comes from your heart, and I applaud you for that. But out of love and concern let me ask you, how is your heart?

PEOPLE FLOCK TO WHAT IS NEW, BUT THEY CONNECT TO THE TRUTH.

"The truth is that we were given music so that we would make the world a better place. Does not the ancient scriptures say to do all things decent and in order? Music for peace means lining up the sound of peace with words of peace. Did you hold up the fruit and begin to speak before knowing what to say? Did you hold the fruit at the right level? Did you make sure your music was in line with the truth?" Otto asked.

"No, our boss told us what to say," Menik replied.

"Your boss? Who is he?" Otto asked.

"He is the man counting the money over there," said Tad, as they pointed to a tall, slender man standing in the corner. "His name is Luc. That name is supposed to be short for something. He moved here because he lost his old job as Chief Musician. Luc is a good boss. He gives us money and music to be written, while Menik and I stand around and eat sound-fruit all day."

THIS, TOO, IS THE NATURE OF MUSIC

Music in the Garden of Good and Evil

Part 2

Music in the City of ID

INTRODUCTION

THESE ARE THE TALES OF OTTO, THE CHIEF MUSIC TEACHER of the Garden of Good and Evil.

Upon receiving the title of Chief Music Teacher, Otto set out into the world to spread the secrets of music that would bring the world a higher level of musical joy. Otto represents the transformation from a student of music to the teacher of musical secrets. Please understand this:

THE POWERS OF MUSIC NEVER WERE INTENDED TO BE KEPT SECRET.

No, the gardener never intended to keep the powers of music hidden from the world. No, my friend, this was a plot of the Evil One. The Evil One knows how to shed light on what he wants you to see. Think long about this. The Evil One needs the truth about music to be a secret, so that the world does not know when he is being musically deceitful. Remember, the Evil One is the great deceiver.

YOU CAN CLOSE YOUR EYES BUT YOUR EARS ARE

ALWAYS OPEN.

But wait! What form of deception could the Evil One have mastered? What was the Evil One's job before he was banished from his Master's kingdom?

Chief Musician!

The Evil One is not only a master of music, he is a master of musical deception. By keeping the principles of music a secret, the Evil One can guide music for his own purposes and at his will. The question is: *Can Otto make a difference in the world, or is it too late?*

These are the tales of a traveler turned teacher. These are the tales of the secrets not meant to be secret. These are the tales of music.

CHAPTER 1

OTTO'S TRAVELS TOOK HIM INTO STRANGE LANDS FULL OF sounds of woe and confusion. The spreading of divine musical knowledge has been a blessing to many people. But there was one city in his travels that proved to be the most memorable of all, the City of Id. Let's read about it.

Otto walked into the heart of the City of Id singing, "Order my steps. Order my steps in Your Word."

Soon Otto encountered a music peddler. "Sir, I can put beautiful music to your words of praise for a cheap price. The city will adore you. You will be famous. Nobody will be able to resist your music. Just eat of this fruit," said the peddler, pointing to his basket.

"Your offer is very interesting, kind sir, but do not the ancient words of wisdom tell us to guard our ears against words of evil?" Otto asked.

"Yes," the peddler responded.

"Then should I not also guard myself against music that cannot be so easily guarded against?" Otto asked.

The music peddler held a minor sound-fruit in the air, and angrily shouted, "This is my sound-fruit! You are a fool and your breath smells of cheese. Be gone, be gone, be gone, if you please!"

"Try your best, music peddler. Try to deceive me with your music. But alas, I know the secrets of music. I will expose you, *YOU SNAKE*, for the deceiver you are. Be gone at once!" Otto shouted boldly.

At that moment the peddler of music fell to the ground and turned into a snake.

"Hissssstory repeats itself, and you will one day eat the fruit," hissed the snake, as he slithered away.

Startled by the meeting with the snake, Otto took a deep breath, and thought, "This entire city must be the second Garden of Good and Evil. It's funny; every time I turn around there is a snake trying to jump up and *bite me*."

"Butter! Get your fresh butter! Fresh butter for sale!" A voice loudly proclaimed, as if a king were approaching.

"Young man, where are all of the musicians in the city?" Otto asked.

"Why, where else would musicians be but in the temple? Just follow the olive-brick road and listen for the music. If the road becomes yellow, then you have gone to far," the young vendor replied.

"Thank you, kind sir. Here is some money. Go and buy yourself some coffee beans. Grind them up, boil them in water, and serve the liquid in cups. Name the new drink after the bucking stars, and the people of the city will chase you down the street to buy every cup you can make," said Otto. And with that display of gratitude Otto began his walk down the olive brick road.

CHAPTER 2

As Otto got closer to the temple, he heard words accompanied by strange music. Otto heard music that was meant for good but did not sound good at all.

Upon entering the temple walls, Otto quickly found the musicians to be inconsistent with their music. The musicians were speaking words of peace and love into sound-fruit that were planted for despair and hardship.

When the music stopped, Otto stepped forward and said, "My, my, what blessed words you have to fill the air of the temple."

"Thank you, kind sir," replied the musicians.

"And what powerful sounds you have. The sounds really fill the room with music so strong that it penetrates the heart, mind, and soul," Otto added.

"You are most kind," the head musician said. "Are you a musician?"

"I am but a humble gardener," Otto replied. "But please tell me, if you will, what kind of music are you creating?"

The head musician proudly replied, "We are making music of praise and joy with sound-fruit."

With a smile, Otto said, "Wonderful, I am so pleased that you know the secret knowledge of the sound-fruit!"

"Foolish man, there is no secret knowledge," said one of the musicians. "We were all given talents, and we have plenty of sound-fruit. So we celebrate our joys and desires through music!"

"I mean no offense," Otto humbly said. "Please, let us sit and share wisdom. I am always eager to learn."

"Just come to the temple tonight. You will hear that all of the people will be pleased with our music!" The head musician proclaimed.

And the musicians turned their attention back to their rehearsal. Meanwhile, Otto listened to the musicians rehearse, all the while knowing the errors of their ways.

"I finally understand that famous saying 'forgive them Father, for they know not what they do,'" Otto thought, as he shook his head.

As night fell on the city, the people poured into the temple to celebrate through music. The music was already playing, and the spirit in the room was high. All of the sudden, a sound was released from the musicians that brought sadness to the congregation. The spirit of the room had changed.

The congregation began to cry out, "Why is this? Why did the spirit change when we were celebrating with all of our hearts? Oh, what have we done?"

"I do not know," replied the head musician, "We were playing music and rejoicing with all of our hearts. Why? Oh why did the spirit change?"

At that point, Otto stood up in the back of the temple, and exclaimed, "I might know why the spirit changed!"

"Why, why, why!" The congregation shouted.

"I am not sure you want to hear the reason," Otto said.

"Please tell us! Why did the spirit change?" The head musician asked.

Otto stood for a moment, looked over the eyes of the people, and said, "Because you told it to change."

CHAPTER 3

"Quiet this nonsense! How dare you blaspheme in the temple! I do not have the power to change the spirit," shouted the head musician.

"And yet under your own handiwork, the spirit did change," Otto replied.

"No, No! We spoke praise and joy into the sound-fruit. We have the basket of fruit right here. It was ripe and ready for music. Why did the spirit change from praise and joy to a strange feeling that brought the people to sadness? Why?" The head musician asked.

Otto took a step back, put his hand under his chin, and said, "Could you have perhaps been using the wrong sound-fruit?"

"There are not different kinds of sound-fruit," said the head musician.

"Oh, there are many. And all of the sound-fruit have specific meanings and uses," replied Otto. "I could share with you the ways of the sound-fruit if you would like. I was taught the secrets of music in the Garden of Good and Evil."

The eyes of the people grew wide. "The garden is where all of the fruit come from. If you will be so kind as to share with us, then we will listen," the head musician replied, and all of the other musicians agreed.

Otto was touched by their humble attitudes. So he agreed to explain the meanings of each sound-fruit: major, minor, transitions, confusion, and faith. Just as Percy taught Otto in the Garden of Good and Evil, Otto wanted to teach these musicians.

Otto continued, "Who among you is willing to become workers in the vineyard? Who among you is willing to dig for the truth? Let those among you willing to do so step forward and learn with me.

"May your hearts and minds be ready to become Disciples of Music. Always seek guidance so that we may better learn how to bring joy to the world."

Then Otto sat on the floor and began to speak to the new Disciples of Music. "My brothers and sisters, you are now Disciples of Music. I will share with you the secrets of music, as it was given to me in the Garden of Good and Evil. Remember, the Garden of Good and Evil was planted by the Creator. I give you the secrets of music, so you can make the world a better place."

Otto took a rock from his pocket and said in a low and convicted voice, "To do this...to really take this music to another level, do you know what you need to do?"

No one said a word. Everyone was standing with a

focused stare, as they waited for the answer.

"You *all* must elevate your minds." Otto raised the rock in the air level by level. "Just as the view from a mountain top is different than the view from the valley below, so is the view of music different when your mind is elevated. Music, just like life, is different when you elevate your thinking. It is my wish that you all elevate your minds to what you are about to hear. What I am about to share with you will change your life and change how you think about the music in your life. Remember these eternal words of ancients:

AS A MAN THINKETH, SO IS HE

"Your music is an expression of your thoughts. As your thoughts about music are, so is your music. Your music will mirror your thoughts, just as your life mirrors your thoughts.

"Think of it like this. As we know, the spirit of good should lead a teacher. But even if that spirit leads the teacher, a teacher should still study the ancient wisdom, prepare the lesson to be taught, and do everything to ensure that the student understands the lesson clearly. The teacher is a vessel of knowledge, who makes sure the lesson fits the knowledge."

"It is apparent that a good and wise teacher must do a lot of thinking, but that thinking must be led by the truth, because as a man thinketh, so is he. There are many things that go into making music. There is the preparation of the sounds, the message in the words, and the spirit within the musician which shapes the way the musician thinks about the music. It is not the case that the spirit alone makes the music, but it is the spirit of the mind that guides the way you think about music. What you think is what you create. Your music is the sum total of your thoughts. That is what makes music so powerful."

AS A MAN THINKETH, SO IS HE

CHAPTER 4

Otto continued his instruction with this admonition:
"You must maintain a life of principles by aligning your words with your actions."

"Why is that so important to music?" One student asked in confusion.

"Applying aligning your music to the message is what the music needs to reach the amount of people it is designed to reach. If you do this, your music will become the vehicle which drives your message to the heart of the people. Music is designed to penetrate the heart," Otto responded. "Do you not always strive to line your actions with your words, your words with your thoughts, and your thoughts with your message?" Otto asked.

"Yes!" The students replied.

"Is it not also the will for everything in your life to be in line with the principles of truth?" Asked Otto.

"Yes, I believe that with my whole heart," many people replied.

"So can we all agree that to be in truth's will is to be in total alignment?" Otto asked.

"Yes, we can agree," they answered.

"Then answer me this," Otto said, as he noticed the new Disciples of Music fixed on his every word. "Is your music of words and sounds a product of your actions?"

"But of course," they replied.

"Then could we agree that your music should line up with your actions, and your actions should line up with your words, and your words should line up with your thoughts, and your thoughts should line up with the Spirit of Truth?" Otto boldly asked.

"Of course! My music should always follow the words. My words should always chase the message. And my message should always be led the Spirit of Truth," the head musician shouted. "Oh, we have been so foolish!"

"Be not hard on yourself. The reason you feel this way is because your view of music is elevating. Your understanding of music has a new foundation to stand on. Your love for the people will now be your strength on your quest for musical understanding. Come now. Let us dig in the true Garden of Good and Evil. Let us dig in your hearts and minds, *The Inner Garden*. That is where you will find what ancient wisdom calls the real fruit, *The Fruit of the Spirit*.

THE TRUE GARDEN OF GOOD AND EVIL IS WITHIN YOU!

CHAPTER 5

"NOW WATCH THIS," OTTO SAID AS HE POINTED TO A SOUND-fruit in the basket of the musicians. "This one is called a major sound-fruit. Its good side is activated by words such as:

LOVE
PRAISE
CELEBRATION
JOY
HAPPINESS
PEACE

"Its evil side is activated by words such as:

BOASTFULNESS
PRIDE
GREED

"The two sides of the fruit are where the Good and Evil are found. The choice is up to you, as to which side you will activate."

Otto then turned to the eldest musician, and said,

"I would like you to clear your mind, take a deep breath, and begin to think about the fruit of the spirit, as it is described by the ancient wisdom: *The fruit of the spirit is love, joy, peace, patience, kindness, faithfullness, gentleness, self-control. . ."*

The eldest musician did so until the fruit of the spirit filled his heart.

"Now, please pick up the major sound-fruit, the yellow one, and speak the words that have filled your heart. Speak of love, joy, and peace!" Otto said excitedly.

The eldest musician raised the major sound-fruit in the air, and said, "I love Thee. With You on the throne of grace, there is joy. With You on the throne of my heart, there is peace."

When he spoke those words into the major sound-fruit, the fruit blossomed a beautiful sound into the air. The people in the room were moved deeply by its glowing beauty. The people felt the sound of pure love. It was sweet and soothing unto the ear.

Otto then addressed the Disciples of Music with these words. "Do you see it? Can you hear it? This is the nature of music. Music is a gift to be used to make the world a better place. Music is so wonderful, because it has the ability to fill us with the same love that we put into to creating it. The power is so strong that even an evil man has the ability to make music that can bring joy and happiness to all that are touched by its sounds."

The musicians stood in awe, as their hearts were filled with joy and adoration.

Otto looked over their amazed faces, and said, "You have heard the right way. Now you will hear sounds that are out of place. These are sounds that do not line up with the words. This is music that fights with the spirit, rather than ushering in the spirit."

The musicians focused intently on Otto's every word, as he continued his teachings. "It is not what goes into the body that defiles you, it is what comes out. The words that come out of you must be pure and so must your thoughts. For out of the heart, the mouth speaks into the music."

Otto looked into the basket of sound-fruit again, and said, "Head musician, would you be so kind as to pick up this red sound-fruit and speak of love, joy, and peace like the eldest musician did."

The head musician did as he was requested. At once the fruit blossomed into a foul sound to the ears. The hearts of the people became heavy and sad.

"Please teacher, let me try again," asked the head musician.

Otto replied, "Not to worry. You picked up a minor sound-fruit. It is not made to give sounds of love."

Otto picked up the major sound-fruit, and said, "Love, joy, and peace!" And at once love filled the room, joy filled their hearts, and peace was restored.

Otto said, "These are the gifts of music. Behold the beauty of the sound-fruit, just as nature intended."

One after the other, major sound-fruit were released by Otto. Everyone in the room began to rejoice and give thanks for the gift of music.

"You see, in music there is no shortage of joy, pain, love, or hate. Those qualities are as abundant as air, warm as fire, refreshing as water, and nourishing as the earth. You just need to choose the right sound to follow your words. Then you will never go wrong. Today's lesson is now over. Tomorrow, meet me in the gardens of the temple, and there I will give you more secrets of music," announced Otto.

IT IS NOT WHAT GOES INTO THE BODY THAT DEFILES YOU, IT IS WHAT COMES OUT OF IT.

Chapter 6

The next day all of the Disciples of Music met in the Majestic Gardens of the Temple. Otto began his lesson, "You see, we were all given the gift of music. All we are doing now is unwrapping this gift, reading the instructions, and putting it together. If the gift is not put together correctly, how do you know if the gift will ever work to its fullest potential?"

"Are you saying that our gifts are not good enough to be used? You are a fool, and I will not listen anymore. I am leaving," shouted one of the musicians, as he stormed out of the garden.

Some of the students tried to stop the angry musician, but Otto said, "Let him go and wish him peace. The musical secrets that I am sharing with you are a way to use your gift to the fullest in order to reach the hearts of the people. Your angry friend is not ready to receive the secrets of the garden. But when he shows himself ready, he will receive them."

As the rest of the musicians settled down, Otto continued. "Gifts are not always given to you completely put together. You must study and refine your gift. *Study to show thyself approved.*

"Know this: The evil one has filled the world with musical undercurrents in order to pull listeners into a deep ocean of confusion. And even if the evil one is not able to bring you down to hell with music, he will surely use musical undercurrents and musical deception to keep you distracted from the joys of life."

CHAPTER 7

OTTO REACHED INTO HIS BAG AND PULLED OUT SOME OF the most important scrolls known to man about music. On the scrolls were writings from the Garden of Good and Evil that told the secrets of music. (Most of these scrolls are reproduced in Part One of this book.)

Otto addressed the Disciples of Music. "In these scrolls are written the secrets of music. Study the lessons well if you want to learn a sacred knowledge:

- The Meanings of the Sound-Fruit
- The Doctrine of Sound Combination
- The Ten Tablets
- The Parables

I will leave these scrolls with you, so that you may study them in the days that I am away."

Otto then left the city to travel back to the Garden of Good and Evil, a journey of three days.

Upon reaching the Garden, Otto looked for Percy to tell of the good news of his travels. "Percy, Percy. Where are you?" He called.

"I am in the center of the garden," Percy replied.

In the center of the Garden Percy was pruning trees that bore new sound-fruit, fruit that Otto had never seen.

"These are truly beautiful sound-fruit, Percy. I have never seen such beauty. Why have I never seen them?" Otto asked.

Percy replied, "Because these trees were planted just today. These trees were planted bearing full fruit. I asked the Creator to reveal what these fruit were. And I heard a powerful voice say, 'This is the *Fruit of the Spirit*'. He is a truly a living creator; I know this because He brings life."

"How is it used?" Otto asked.

"The Creator said that the Fruit of the Spirit cannot be released by man. The Fruit of the Spirit will be set free by the power that connects all people. Let us be thankful for the many blessing of music," Percy said, as they bowed their heads in prayer.

After the prayer, Percy asked about Otto's journeys, "Well, did you find the City of Id to be full of Egos and Super Egos?"

Otto replied, "Very funny! You haven't lost your sense of humor. Well, there were many egos in the city. But my students are very humble and are learning at a fast pace. Not everyone wanted to learn the secrets, but all those who stayed were teachable."

Otto told Percy about meeting the music peddler and finding the temple. He told about seeing his old friends, Menik and Tad, and how they had been tricked by the Evil One, who now had control over them. Percy and Otto spent the rest of the day talking about old times.

After one week Otto packed his bags in preparation for the return journey. Percy hugged Otto and gave his blessings for peaceful travel. Then Percy pulled a beautiful sound-fruit, the *Fruit of the Spirit*, from the sacred tree. "Take this new fruit with you. It has a power unlike the world has ever known. Go back to the City of Id and teach the people. Be well, and go in peace."

"Thank you. How does it work?" Otto asked in excitement.

"Do not worry, my friend. When the time is right, the Fruit of the Spirit will teach *you*."

Otto gently placed this special fruit in his bag and left the garden for his three-day journey back to the city.

CHAPTER 8

ONCE BACK AT THE TEMPLE, OTTO WAS GREETED BY THE Disciples of Music. "We have studied, just as you have told us. We all want to learn more," said the head musician.

Otto looked over the faces of the musicians, and said, "I am overjoyed by such a gracious welcome. I am eager to get started. Let us gather in the garden."

The Disciples of Music poured out toward the Majestic Garden of the Temple and sat near Otto. Otto next spoke these words, and the disciples wrote them down on scrolls. These scrolls contained the many of the same words spoken by Otto on that day in the temple gardens:

Scrolls of Otto
The Majestic Gardens of the Temple
The City of Id

YOU ARE NEVER TO EAT OF THE FRUIT. THOSE WHO DO EAT OF THE FRUIT ARE GIVEN OVER TO EVIL.

WORDS AND MUSICAL SOUNDS ARE LIKE THE CURRENTS OF AN OCEAN. THE LYRICS ARE THE TOP CURRENTS AND THE SOUNDS ARE THE UNDERCURRENT. THE TOP CURRENT IS THE ONE THAT GUIDES YOU AND THE UNDERCURRENT IS THE ONE THAT PULLS YOU. MAKE SURE YOUR MUSIC FLOWS IN THE SAME DIRECTION AS YOUR LYRICS, OTHERWISE YOU WILL BE PULLED IN A DIFFERENT DIRECTION.

MUSIC IS SOUND THAT IS SHAPED BY THE MUSICIAN. MUSIC IS THE FIRE THAT CAN BRING WARMTH TO A FAMILY IN THE WINTER OR BURN DOWN A VILLAGE DURING A TIME OF DROUGHT. LEARN TO CONTROL THE BURNING FIRES OF SOUND.

MUSIC IS LIKE PAINTING A PICTURE. THE CHILD GRABS A PAINTBRUSH AND PAINTS BRIGHT RED ON A SCROLL, BUT ALL THE WHILE THE CHILD THINKS THE COLOR IS BLUE. NO MATTER HOW HARD THAT CHILD SHOUTS "BLUE," THE PAINT WILL ALWAYS BE RED. MAKE SURE YOU ARE NOT THE SHOUTING CHILD. MAKE SURE YOU ARE NOT THE ONE SHOUTING JOY WHILE HOLDING A MINOR SOUND-FRUIT OF PAIN.

THERE WAS ONCE A MAN OF PEACE WHO WANTED TO BECOME A DOCTOR, BECAUSE HE HAD THE GIFT OF HEALING. BUT TO BECOME A GOOD DOCTOR HE HAD TO STUDY MEDICINE. SO HE WENT TO SCHOOL AND STUDIED MEDICINE WITH VERY SKILLED DOCTORS. WHEN HE WAS FINISHED, HE WAS A SKILLED DOCTOR WHO HAD THE GIFT OF HEALING AND WAS LED BY THE SPIRIT OF TRUTH. THIS, TOO, IS WHAT IT MEANS TO BE A WELL STUDIED AND GIFTED MUSICIAN. STUDY TO SHOW YOURSELF APPROVED. BE LED BY THE SPIRIT OF TRUTH, AND YOU WILL BE A SPIRIT-LED MUSICIAN.

MUSIC HOLDS WITHIN IT THE POWER OF SUGGESTION. IF YOU MEDITATE ON THE WORDS OF A SONG LONG ENOUGH, YOUR THOUGHTS WILL BEGIN TO HARMONIZE WITH THE SONG. THEN YOUR THOUGHTS WILL BECOME ACTIONS. THIS, TOO, IS THE NATURE OF MUSIC.

These are the only scrolls left from the temple gardens. Many other stories were passed down through the ages by word of mouth.

Otto continued. "Is believing in wisdom all there is to being a wise person, or do you need to study the wisdom of the ages? Would it be good enough to practice being wise one day of the week and be foolish the other six? No, of course not. Wise people spend tireless days and sleepless nights studying the ancient words of wisdom.

"Well, musicians study music and wise musicians use wisdom in placing the words with the right sounds. First, speak the words of love into the major sound-fruit, then love will cause the fruit to blossom into a beautiful glowing sound. The music will reach all those who can hear, thus spreading love through sound."

IF A PICTURE IS WORTH
A THOUSAND WORDS, THEN
MUSIC TELLS THE
REST OF THE STORY.

Chapter 9

"Otto, although you have explained this, I still do not understand how the transition sound-fruit is used. We have studied the scroll's definitions, but we want to know why the transition fruit is needed. I can see the need for the major sound-fruit:

> Love
>
> Joy
>
> Peace
>
> Praise
>
> Good

I, also, see the need for the minor sound-fruit:

> Pain
>
> Trials
>
> Tribulations
>
> Hardship
>
> Evil

But why are there more fruit? Why do we need transition fruit?" The head musician asked.

Otto scratched his chin, and replied, "Good question, my friend. Come. Follow me to the stream." The group followed Otto down to the stream. Otto bent down and put his hand in the water. "This stream is crystal clear and moving towards the temple. The water feels good to the touch and is good to drink. The canal on the other side of the temple is dirty, and is flowing away from the temple. The clean water is flowing to the temple drinking wells. The dirty water is going to the ditches for the pigs to drink.

"Now, follow me closely. The clear, moving water is like a transition sound-fruit. It is the good water of sound flowing towards a reservoir of happiness." Otto took a sip of the clean water.

"The dirty water represents an alternate sound-fruit flowing towards the ditches of sad sounds." Otto pointed to the dirty canal. He then grabbed a leaf and threw it into the water. "You see, like a leaf in a stream, sound is always moving. And like water, if sound does not move, it will stagnate. Like any person's life, music is often in a state of transition. Music is either:

Happy

Becoming Happy

Sad

Becoming Sad

This is the nature of music. As Disciples of Music, your music must tell the story of Joy and Pain and how we get there."

"Why is it so important that we follow principles when making music?" Asked the youngest musician.

"Because art imitates life," replied Otto. "So good music is imitating a good life. There are good times and bad times, ups and downs. But the bad times are not necessarily evil. Bad times are often things we have to go through to get to a better place."

Many weeks had passed by and the Disciples of Music finally became ready to move on to the next level of knowledge.

"Now it is time to learn how the nature of man connects to the nature of music," Otto said. "So learn these scrolls and use them well." Although there were two scrolls on the Nature on Music, only one has survived. It is printed below:

Music and the Nature of Man

KNOW THYSELF, BECAUSE ART IMITATES LIFE.
SOME PEOPLE ARE DRAWN TO MINOR SOUNDS
BECAUSE THEIR LIVES ARE FILLED WITH
HARDSHIPS AND PAIN.
ART IMITATES LIFE
SOME PEOPLE ARE DRAWN TO TRANSITION
SOUNDS BECAUSE THEIR LIVES ARE ALWAYS IN
TRANSITION.
SOME PEOPLE ARE DRAWN TO FAITH SOUNDS
(SUSPENSIONS) BECAUSE THEY WANT TO BE
INSPIRED.
SOME PEOPLE ARE DRAWN TO MAJOR SOUNDS
BECAUSE THEY LONG FOR THE FEELINGS OF
PEACE AND LOVE.

Otto then pointed out the most important fact of music. "You must be led by the spirit of truth or you will fall into the musical desires of your flesh."

"Are you saying that music is a temptation?" Asked the youngest musician.

"No, no, no my friend. The flesh craves certain sounds, and certain sounds can become addictive," Otto replied. "But let us not forget that the Evil One is crafty. And never forget that the Evil One was the Chief Musician before he was cast out of his Master's house. So how much of the powerful effects of music do you think the Evil One knows?"

The head musician replied, "If the Evil One was the Chief Musician, then he must know all knowledge of music. And if music has the power to affect us and change the spirit, then the Evil One could be using music to tempt the cravings of our flesh!"

"Exactly!" Otto said, "The Evil One is the great deceiver. He makes you think that all of the music you listen to is perfectly fine, and you just reply, 'Everything feels so good, that it must be good for me'. You would say this because your cravings were being fed by pleasurable sounds. Does this not sound like a meeting of a seller of potions and his addict?" Otto asked.

"Yes it does. The Evil One is supplying people with the sounds they crave," replied one of the women.

"And understand this!" Otto said, as he paused to

focus his attention on the group. "*The Evil One uses the same sounds that you crave against you, to control you, to have dominion over you!*" The Disciples of Music all gasped at what they were hearing.

"So know thyself. If you feel a musical craving of the flesh that is contrary to what you know is right, do not feed the sound. Starve that sound, so that it may become weak and die. An ancient wise man said 'I die daily,' and you will have to do the same with your music. The spirit and the flesh both crave music. Would it not be good to feed the spirit and deny the flesh?"

Otto turned his attention to a passing bird and continued. "If you are a musician, should you not know this? If you listen to any music, should you not know this? This week I would like you all to fast from music. Abstain from all sounds of music to purify yourselves. Your ears are toxic. Cleanse your minds with the words of peace. Read the ancient words of wisdom without ceasing and search for understanding." For the next three months Otto taught the Disciples of Music more about the secrets of the Garden of Good and Evil.

IF YOU ARE A MUSICIAN, SHOULD YOU NOT KNOW THIS?

IF YOU LISTEN TO ANY MUSIC, SHOULD YOU NOT KNOW THIS?

CHAPTER 10

MANY MONTHS HAD PASSED, AND THE DISCIPLES OF Music grew like wild vines in their knowledge.

"This is the day that each of you will reveal your music to the rest of the Disciples," Otto told the group. "Throughout our time together, you have studied:

> The Meanings of the Sound-Fruit
> The Doctrine of Sound Combination
> The Ten Tablets of Music
> The Parables of the Garden

"You have learned the three things it takes to be a Disciple of Music:

> Be Ye Led by Peace
> Be Ye Rooted in Truth
> Be Ye Wise in Your Musical Knowledge

"So who will be first to share their music with the people?" Otto asked.

"I will be the first," said the head musician. He then carefully placed five sound-fruit on the table. Once the fruit were arranged, the head musician picked up a major sound-fruit, and said: "The Beauty of a Thousand Hills Flows through Your Heart!"

The fruit at once burst into a glorious sound and a brilliant color.

The musician then picked up more sound-fruit:

(Minor)	*In my pain and trials*
(Transition)	*I am changing*
(Major)	*Into a man of peace.*
(Minor)	*In my pain and trials*
(Transition)	*I am pressing on to*
(Major)	*Victory!*

One by one the sound-fruit burst into all of the glorious sounds of the nature and glowed all of the mesmerizing colors: sunset orange, sky blue, ruby red, and yellow rose.

All of the disciples shouted praises! Then the people standing by the doors came into the temple to hear the glorious music. The music touched the hearts of the people, as the people began to be filled with the joy of sound.

"Keep going, more songs. Let us give the gift of music to the people!" Otto shouted with joy.

All of the sudden a loud rumble swept across the city. Otto's bag became warm and glowed. It slowly opened by itself. Then the new fruit from the Garden of Good and Evil flew out of Otto's bag and into the air. Otto looked in awe. "Glory, glory, glory! It is the *Fruit of the Spirit!*"

And then in a flash of majestic lights the Fruit of the Spirit bursts into all of the colors of the rainbow and all of the sounds that the world has ever heard. The sound of this fruit was a sweet joy released through the tears of the hearts of the people!

The glorious sound of the *Fruit of the Spirit* filled the temple walls and passed through the doors like a mighty rushing wind into the streets. And all in the City of Id came to be filled with joy and peace.

Even Otto's old friends, Tad and Menik, came into the temple and with one sound were freed from the Evil One's hold. Otto hugged his friends and then spoke to all the people in a mighty voice:

AND YE SHALL KNOW THE TRUTH, AND THE TRUTH SHALL SET YOU FREE!

Volume I of III

EPILOGUE

Percy, the Gardener in the Garden of Good and Evil, prepared me, so that I would share the secrets of music with the world. I wanted people to believe in the power of something that they could not see. You cannot see music, but you can feel it.

Even if you do not make music, you are affected by music just by listening to it. This is not a story designed to teach you about the technical aspects of music. This story is designed to let you know that music has the power to affect your mind and soul.

Music has the power to make you feel something that you never even knew existed. It is a powerful force that cannot be reasoned with, because it chooses no sides. We were given music as a gift the bring joy to the world. So be thankful for the *Gift of Music*, because music has the power to lift the spirit and give joy to everyone it reaches. Although I will not always be here, I am leaving these scrolls so that it may tell the story. Now the secrets of music are in your trusted hands to share with the world.

Otto

About the Author

Lorne Lee has an extensive history as a music professor, composer, band director, Minister of Music, clinician, consultant, and adjudicator. Lorne has held the positions of Director of Bands and Assistant Professor of Music at Johnson C. Smith University in Charlotte, NC, Associate Director of Bands at Livingstone College in Salisbury, NC, and Director of Bands and Assistant Professor of Music at Savannah State University in Savannah, GA.

Lorne Lee earned his Master of Music degree from Howard University in Washington, D.C. and his Bachelor of Music degree from The University of Central Oklahoma in Edmond, OK.

www.ingramcontent.com/pod-product-compliance
Lightning Source LLC
Chambersburg PA
CBHW031320060726